LMS
STEAM PORTRAIT

LMS
STEAM PORTRAIT

BRIAN STEPHENSON

LONDON

IAN ALLAN LTD

Contents

RIGHT: By 1930 several LNWR 'Claughton' 4-6-0s were transferred to the Midland Division for working between St Pancras, Leeds and Carlisle following the introduction of the 'Royal Scot' Class 4-6-0s on the West Coast main line. Here a Midland Class 2P 4-4-0 pilots an unidentified 'Claughton' with an up express seen approaching Elstree c1931. *Lens of Sutton*

First published 1985

ISBN 0 7110 1523 6

Published by Ian Allan Ltd, Shepperton, Surrey; and printed by Ian Allan Printing Ltd at their works at Coombelands in Runnymede, England

TITLE PAGE OVERLEAF: Fowler LMS three-cylinder Class 4P compound 4-4-0 No 1097 toils up the 1 in 176 past Mill Hill with the heavy 1.45pm St Pancras-Leeds express in June 1926.
F. R. Hebron/Rail Archive Stephenson

COVER: 'Patriot' No 5983 climbs away from Nottingham with the up 'Thames-Forth Express' in 1933/4.
Painting by George F. Heiron, from a photograph by T. G. Hepburn

Introduction

This book has been produced in answer to all those LMS enthusiasts who have been hoping for a reprint of my *LMS Albums* number two and number three first published in 1971 and 1973. As this is no longer technically possible it was decided to take the best material from the two Albums and to add some new photographs to form this tribute to LMS steam.

As recalled in the Introduction to LMS Album number two, that with two historic rivals included in the infant LMS its early years were bound to be far from smooth. On the locomotive front Crewe was already far from happy with the outcome of the amalgamation of the London & North Western Railway with the Lancashire & Yorkshire Railway whereby George Hughes of the LYR became Chief Mechanical Engineer of the enlarged LNWR. A further blow fell on Crewe after the grouping in 1923, although Hughes was chosen as CME of the new Company he was near retiring age, and in 1925 he was succeeded by Sir Henry Fowler who had been CME of the Midland Railway since 1909.

Fowler who had been quietly continuing the MR small engine policy at Derby immediately saw to the mass construction of his MR designs for use on most of the LMS system. Thus the three-cylinder compound 4-4-0s were soon to be found at work on the West Coast main line much to the dismay of Crewe. Nothing could have been more calculated to cause resentment than the introduction of what was basically a 1905 MR design when the so called 'Premier Line' had such magnificent engines as the four-cylinder 'Claughtons'.

Midland influence did not only apply to locomotives, new rolling stock was on the whole based on Midland designs, though when it came to sleeping and dining cars it was LNWR designs that were followed at first. The locomotive power class system of classifying engine power in relation to loads was pure Midland. In 1928 the letters 'F' for freight and 'P' for passenger were added to the power class numbers and it is the post 1928 classes that I have used throughout this book. Lastly but by no means least the livery adopted by the LMS was Midland even to the large numerals on the locomotive tenders, all originally part of the MR train control system. At Crewe this did not work very well as tenders were never considered as married to one engine so it was sometimes possible to see an engine with a tender bearing another engine's number. After applying the crimson lake livery at first, Crewe stopped repainting engines in LMS livery due, so it was said, to a reorganisation in the works, and many engines were returned to traffic after repair in LNWR black with their old numberplates. Even in later years after crimson lake had been dropped for all but the most important engines, 'Claughton' 4-6-0s still continued to appear in black, though with the correct LMS number and insignia but with North Western lining out on the buffer beams and occasionally on the tenders!

George Hughes had before his retirement, multiplied his LYR design of four-cylinder 4-6-0 for use on the West Coast main line. He also initiated the Horwich Mogul design which appeared in 1926 unhappily matched with a Fowler tender, the engine was pure Horwich and a fine machine at that. In Scotland the Glasgow & South Western stock was quickly displaced by Fowler 4-4-0s. Compounds appeared on the Caledonian while on the Highland at first the only new engines in any quantity were the Horwich 'Crabs'. By 1927 things had come to such a pass on the West Coast main line that Fowler had to hurriedly seek the help of the North British Locomotive Company in turning out the first 50 'Royal Scot'

class 4-6-0s. He saw to the excellent Class 4P 2-6-4Ts and the ultimate rebuilt 'Claughtons' that were later known as 'Patriots'. On the debit side were the dreadfully undershod Class 7F 0-8-0s and Beyer-Garratt 2-6-0+0-6-2Ts, the later would have been so much better if the design had been left completely in the hands of Beyer, Peacock though it should be remembered it was relatively early days in the development of Garratts.

Thus the powerful Derby MR influence did not really end until 1932 when William Stanier was appointed CME of the LMS. He brought many features of Swindon practice to the LMS such as domeless low superheat boilers that were not to prove as successful as on the GWR. He turned out the first LMS Pacific design, *The Princess Royal* in June 1933 and went on to produce his own taper boiler version of the Horwich Mogul and Class 4P 2-6-4T, albeit with three cylinders at first. Most notable was the mixed traffic 4-6-0, the famous 'Black Five' and Class 8F 2-8-0 which were to be built in large numbers to help see the LMS through World War 2 and beyond to the end of steam on British Railways in 1968.

Stanier was appointed to a wartime ministerial post in 1942 and Charles Fairburn acted as CME until 1944 when he was appointed to that post on Stanier's retirement. Meanwhile Stanier designs continued to be built with only minor alterations as the years went by. H. G. Ivatt took over in 1945 and produced three new designs of steam locomotive but perhaps more important he saw to the design and construction of the two main line diesel-electric locomotives Nos 10000 and 10001, the first to run in this country. After nationalisation in 1948 Ivatt remained in charge of London Midland Region mechanical affairs until 1951.

Sadly several of the photographers who so willingly gave me the freedom to use any of their photographs in the original *LMS Albums* have passed away. Particular mention must be made of the late Frank Hebron and Gordon Hepburn who photographed so much of the early LMS and whose photographs form half of this book. I must thank C. R. L. Coles, J. G. Dewing, Neville Fields, L. Hanson and John P. Wilson who also kindly supplied photographs for the original albums and to John L. Smith of Lens of Sutton for some of the new material in this book. Other photographs are by courtesy of the publisher's files. Lastly thanks to Mickey, my wife, who despairs of ever seeing the dining room table clear of photographs and other railway paraphernalia!

BWLS
May 1985

LEFT: The LMS rebuilt 20 'Claughtons' with larger boilers in 1928 and 10 of them were also fitted with Beardmore-Caprotti valve gear. Two of the Caprotti engines, No 5908 *Alfred Fletcher* and 5962, are seen climbing Camden bank with the 6.05pm Euston-Manchester express in 1930.
F. R. Hebron/Rail Archive Stephenson

BELOW: The last 'Claughton' of all to remain in service was large boilered No 6004, formerly named *Princess Louise* until the 'Princess Royal' class Pacific No 6204 appeared with the same name in 1935, passes Kilburn High Road with the 6.15pm Camden-Birmingham goods on 7 June 1939. This was a regular turn for this engine and No 6017 *Breadalbane* at this time when both were allocated to Willesden. No 6004 was withdrawn in 1949, eight years after the previous 'Claughton' withdrawals. *E. R. Wethersett/Real Photographs Co*

BELOW: Bowen-Cooke 'Prince of Wales' Class 4P 4-6-0 No 5765 and a Whale 'Experiment' Class 3P 4-6-0 double-head a northbound goods away from Carnforth in May 1928. The 'Prince of Wales' class, introduced in 1911, were a superheated version of George Whale's 'Experiment' class.
F. R. Hebron/Rail Archive Stephenson

RIGHT: Whale 'Experiment' Class 3P 4-6-0 No 5464 *City of Glasgow* leaves Willesden Junction with an up parcels train on 27 July 1930. Introduced in 1905, the scrapping of this class started in 1925 and all were gone by the end of 1935 swept away by the tide of Stanier 'Black Fives'.
E. R. Wethersett/Real Photographs Co

LEFT: In 1934 all the surviving LNWR express passenger engines numbered between 5000 and 5845 were renumbered by the addition of 20000 to their numbers to avoid duplication with the new Stanier 4-6-0s then coming into traffic. 'Prince of Wales' No 25704 *Scotia* stands in the centre road at Nottingham Midland before working a train to Leicester on a daily turn from Rugby.
J. N. Hall/Rail Archive Stephenson

ABOVE: Whale '19in Goods' Class 4F 4-6-0 No 8852 takes water from Dillicar troughs in the beautiful Lune Gorge with a down freight c1931. There were 170 of these engines built between 1906-9. Three survived to nationalisation and No 8824 was the last LNWR 4-6-0 when withdrawn in 1950 barely outliving the last of the 245 'Prince of Wales' 4-6-0s which went in October 1949.
F. R. Hebron/Rail Archive Stephenson

UPPER LEFT: Whale 'Precursor' Class 3P 4-4-0 No 5263 *Oceanic* pilots 'Royal Scot' class 4-6-0 No 6109 *Royal Engineer* out of Oxenholme for the climb over Grayrigg and Shap with the down 'Royal Scot' in 1929. The 130 'Precursors' were built in 1904-7 and 68 were later superheated.

LOWER LEFT: Another look at the 'Royal Scot', this time the up train passing Tring double-headed by Bowen-Cooke 'George the Fifth' Class 3P 4-4-0 No 5384 *S. R. Graves* and 'Claughton' 4-6-0 No 5958 in 1927. The 'Georges' were a superheated development of the 'Precursor' class and 90 were built at Crewe in 1910-5.

BELOW: Superheated 'Precursor' 4-4-0 No 5310 *Thunderer* climbs Camden bank out of Euston with the 4pm Manchester London Road express in 1930. The engine is in the post 1927 black livery with its number on the cabsides as is No 5263 opposite. The last 'Precursor' went in October 1949 surviving the last 'George the Fifth' by over a year.   *All: F. R. Hebron/Rail Archive Stephenson*

ABOVE: Webb 'Precedent' Class 1P 2-4-0 No 5000 *Princess Beatrice* departs from Nottingham London Road low level with a train for Northampton via the GN&LNW joint line in 1930. The three coaches are of LYR origin. *T. G. Hepburn/Rail Archive Stephenson*

TOP RIGHT: In 1923-4 five 'Waterloo' class 2-4-0s were transferred to the Engineer's Dept for working permanent way trains. They were given the names of the depots to which they were attached and *Engineer Watford*, formerly LNWR No 793 *Martin* which was allocated LMS No 5101, is seen with a down Engineer's train south of Watford Junction c1930. At the grouping there were already three 'Waterloo' and seven 'Samson' 2-4-0s attached to the Engineer's Dept. *F. R. Hebron/Rail Archive Stephenson*

RIGHT: 'Renown' Class 2P 4-4-0 No 5110 *Iron Duke* and Hughes LYR Class 8, LMS 5P, four-cylinder 4-6-0 have just passed Shap summit with an up Manchester express c1930. *Iron Duke* was originally one of F. W. Webb's four-cylinder compound 'Jubilee' class and was rebuilt as a two-cylinder simple 'Renown' in 1924. A total of 70 engines from the 'Jubilee' and 'Alfred the Great' classes were rebuilt in the same manner between 1908 and 1924. They were used mainly as pilot engines and were soon scrapped by the LMS, the last six including *Iron Duke* going in 1931. *LPC/Real Photographs Co*

BELOW: Bowen-Cooke 'G1' Class 6F 0-8-0 No 9196 heads an up goods at Wreay south of Carlisle on 23 December 1938. The 'G1' class was introduced in 1912 and totalled 241 engines including many rebuilt from earlier Webb and Whale 0-8-0s. They were followed by 60 'G2' Class 7F 0-8-0s built by H. P. M. Beames in 1921-2. *E. E. Smith*

UPPER RIGHT: Webb '17in Coal Engine' Class 2F 0-6-0 No 8204 trundles a down local freight through Shrewsbury station, summer 1937. There were 500 of these engines built in 1873-92 of which 227 came into LMS ownership. *E. E. Smith*

LOWER RIGHT: Webb 'Cauliflower' Class 2F 0-6-0 No 8367 enters Fenny Stratford with a Cambridge-Bletchley train, summer 1938. The leading coach is one of the celebrated Clayton MR clerestories, in this case a non-corridor compartment third. The remaining coaches are all Stanier LMS flush sided steel panelled corridor stock which became the hallmark of the LMS in later years. The 310 'Cauliflowers' were built in 1880-1902 and all but two came into LMS stock. *C. R. L. Coles*

LEFT: Webb 5ft 'Watford' Class 2P 0-6-2T No 6871 takes water at Watford Junction in the mid-1930s. Built in 1898-1902 these engines were used on the Euston and Broad Street to Watford local services before electrification was completed in 1922. *C. R. L. Coles*

RIGHT: Webb 5ft 6in Class 1P 2-4-2T No 6624 passes Kinnerton with a Denbigh-Chester fast train c1930. Of the 160 engines in this class built in 1890-7, three were scrapped before the grouping. *LPC/Real Photographs Co*

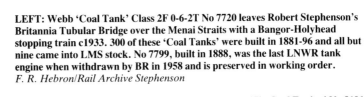

LEFT: Webb 'Coal Tank' Class 2F 0-6-2T No 7720 leaves Robert Stephenson's Britannia Tubular Bridge over the Menai Straits with a Bangor-Holyhead stopping train c1933. 300 of these 'Coal Tanks' were built in 1881-96 and all but nine came into LMS stock. No 7799, built in 1888, was the last LNWR tank engine when withdrawn by BR in 1958 and is preserved in working order.
F. R. Hebron/Rail Archive Stephenson

BELOW: Webb 5ft 6in Class 1P 2-4-2T No 6688 and '17in Coal Engine' No 8191 on shed at Warrington, 26 April 1936. *L. Hanson*

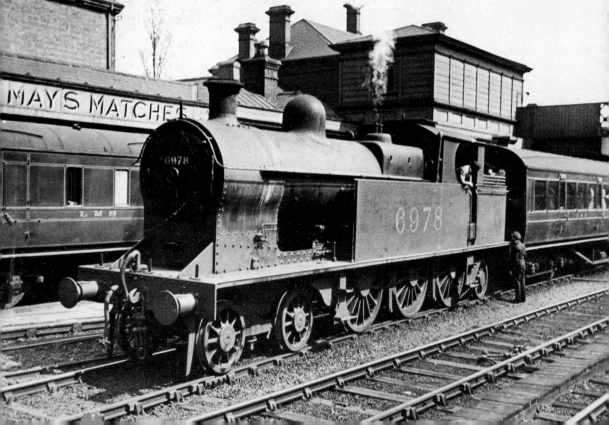

Midland

ABOVE: Veteran Kirtley double-framed Class 1P 2-4-0 No 20012 heads a Cambridge-Kettering train near Cranford on 24 May 1937. Like so many of the 2,925 Midland Railway engines included in LMS stock, it has received various alterations in the course of time. It has been given a Johnson boiler, cab and tender, while Deeley supplied the chimney and smokebox door. It was this last feature that was to spoil the appearance of all the graceful Johnson engines in later years and it remained standard for the MR and LMS until Stanier took over locomotive affairs. There were 29 of these robust engines built in 1866-74 and the last, No 20002, was withdrawn for preservation in 1947. The addition of 20000 to their numbers took place in 1934 to make way for the renumbering of Fowler 2-6-2Ts.
T. G. Hepburn/Rail Archive Stephenson

BELOW: Rebuilt Kirtley Class 1P 2-4-0 No 115 nears Mill Hill with a Bedford-St Pancras train on 13 June 1926. Rebuilt by Johnson there were originally 60 engines in this class built in 1874-75. *F. R. Hebron/Rail Archive Stephenson*

BOTTOM: Johnson Class 1P 6ft 9in 2-4-0 No 20251, fitted with a Belpaire firebox, stands in Bedford station in June 1939. The last of these engines, No 20216 was withdrawn in 1948. *C. R. L. Coles*

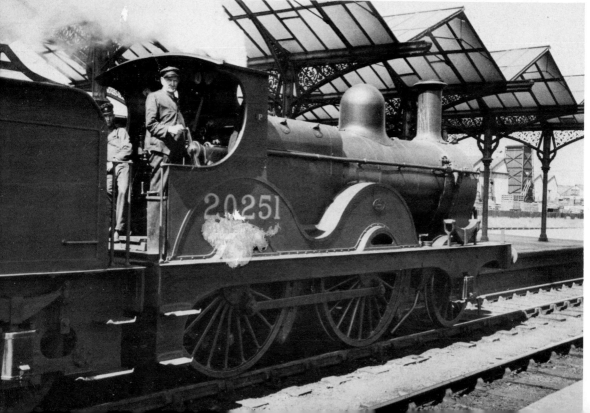

TOP: The pioneer Johnson 4-2-2 No 600, built in 1887 with 7ft 4½in d⟨...⟩ ⟨...⟩en in Nottingham Midland station c1926. It was the only Johnson 'Spinner' to ⟨...⟩ ⟨...⟩ Deeley cab in addition to his ugly smokebox and chimney that marred these beautiful engi⟨...⟩

ABOVE: The most numerous Johnson Singles were the 7ft 6½in drivered version, of which 32 were built. Here resplendent in LMS crimson lake No 641 stand in Nottingham Midland as pilot to a Class 3P 4-4-0 on a St Pancras express in 1926. In all 95 Johnson Singles were built in the period 1887-1900 of five distinct types. *Both: T. G. Hepburn/Rail Archive Stephenson*

ABOVE: Rebuilt Johnson Class 2P 6ft 6in 4-4-0 No 435 leaves Peterborough East with the 5.10pm Leicester train on 12 September 1926. No 435, withdrawn the following year, was one of 55 built in 1893-1900 and were subsequently rebuilt by Deeley from 1905. From 1914 onwards 35 (excluding No 435) were further rebuilt by Henry Fowler with superheated boilers and 7ft driving wheels to conform with his '483' class which themselves were rebuilds of earlier Johnson engines introduced in 1882. Many of these were accountancy rebuilds as little if any of the original engines survived.
F. R. Hebron/Rail Archive Stephenson

UPPER RIGHT: Rebuilt Johnson Class 2P 4-4-0 No 391 leaves Grange-over-Sands with a Barrow-in-Furness-Carnforth train in May 1928. No 391 was one of 15 6ft 6in 4-4-0s built in 1888 and has been rebuilt by Deeley and Fowler with a Belpaire firebox and extended smokebox. This class was to remain saturated and the last was withdrawn in 1952. *F. R. Hebron/Rail Archive Stephenson*

LOWER RIGHT: One of the five Johnson 6ft 9in Class 2P 4-4-0s rebuilt to the '483' class by Fowler in 1923, No 332 leaves New Mills with a Chinley-Marple local on 25 June 1938.
R. D. Pollard/Neville Fields Collection

BELOW: Rebuilt Johnson Class 3P 4-4-0 No 758 leaves Elstree Tunnel with the 1.30pm St Pancras-Sheffield express in 1925. All but seven of these engines built in 1900-05 were rebuilt with superheaters and larger cylinders by Fowler from 1913. *F. R. Hebron/Rail Archive Stephenson*

BOTTOM: Sister engine No 759, in black livery, pilots '483' Class 2P 4-4-0 No 530 on a Manchester-Derby express near Whatstandwell c1930. *LPC/Real Photographs Co*

ABOVE: Deeley Class 4P Compound 4-4-0 No 1012 passes Duffield with a Sheffield-Bristol express c1930. One of the celebrated Clayton 12-wheel clerestory dining cars is next to the engine. These engines retained crimson livery after 1927.
LPC/Real Photographs Co

RIGHT: Another of the 7ft compounds, No 1029 passes Mill Hill with a St Pancras-Leeds express on 13 July 1926. The first Deeley compounds came out in 1905 and were a development of the Smith/Johnson design of 1901. They were all superheated by Fowler from 1913-28.
F. R. Hebron/Rail Archive Stephenson

ABOVE: Kirtley double-framed Class 1F 0-6-0 No 2786 heads a train of coal empties in the late 1920s. Large numbers of these engines were built in 1863-74 and 449 of them came into LMS stock in 1923. *Lens of Sutton*

UPPER RIGHT: Johnson Class 2F 0-6-0 No 3397 at Derby c1926. It was one of 865 Johnson Class 2F 0-6-0s built in 1875-1902. *T. G. Hepburn/Rail Archive Stephenson*

LOWER RIGHT: Many of the Johnson 0-6-0s were rebuilt by Deeley with larger boilers becoming Class 3F. One of these No 3252 is seen fresh from overhaul at Derby on 29 May 1937. *T. G. Hepburn/Rail Archive Stephenson*

ABOVE: Fowler Class 4F 0-6-0 No 3916 leaves Elstree New Tunnel with a down goods in the late 1930s. The first two '4Fs' came out in 1911 but it was not until 1917 that further construction started with a total of 192 built up to 1922. *C. R. L. Coles*

RIGHT: Deeley Class 3F 0-6-0 No 3815 passes through the MSJA platforms at Manchester London Road with a local pick-up freight on 5 April 1938. From 1903 70 engines from No 3765 were built new to Class 3F. *R. D. Pollard/Neville Fields Collection*

LEFT: Fowler Class 4F 0-6-0 No 3927 climbs past Gow Hole sidings with a summer Saturday Llandudno-Sheffield train on 12 August 1939. An LYR brake composite is next to the engine while the rest of train is mostly made up of early LMS corridor stock.

RIGHT: Another '4F', No 3881 rattles downgrade towards New Mills South Junction with a down goods on 2 July 1938. Gow Holes sidings can be seen in the background.
Both: R. D. Pollard/Neville Fields Collection

ABOVE: Johnson Class 1F 0-6-0T No 1805 pauses during shunting in the late 1920s. It is in the pre 1928 plain black freight engine livery with the vermilion backed LMS panel on the bunker sides. There were 280 of these tanks built from 1874. *LPC/Real Photographs Co*

RIGHT: One of the later Johnson Class 3F 0-6-0Ts built in 1899-1902 which were originally numbered 1900-59. Formerly No 1929, No 7229 is beside the coal stage at Kentish Town shed in the late 1930s. It is one of the 30 fitted with condensing apparatus for working through the Metropolitan line tunnels. *T. G. Hepburn/Rail Archive Stephenson*

LEFT: Deeley Class 3P 0-6-4T No 2021 near Whatstandwell with a down goods in the early 1930s. Forty of these tanks were built in 1907 and all had been scrapped by 1939. *F. R. Hebron/Rail Archive Stephenson*

BELOW: Another view of a Deeley 'Flatiron' as No 2000 pilots rebuilt M&GN Class C 4-4-0 No 52 on the Nottingham-Great Yarmouth through train seen passing London Road Junction as it leaves Nottingham on 13 August 1932. *T. G. Hepburn/Rail Archive Stephenson*

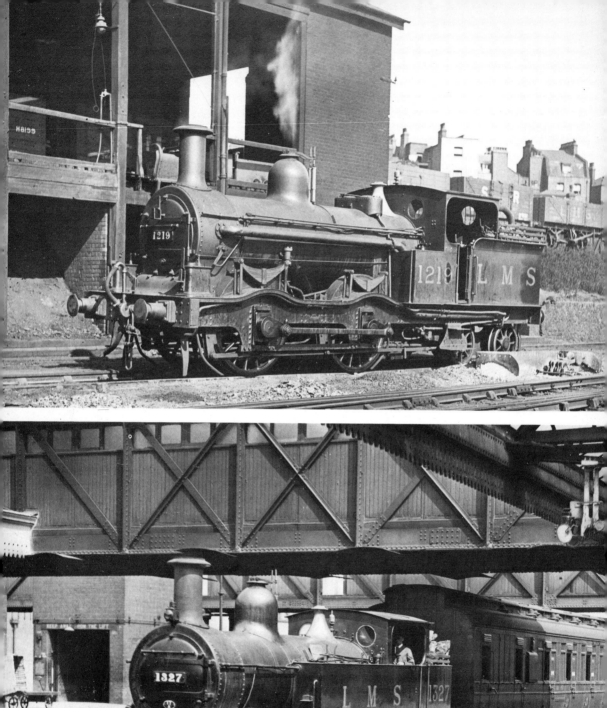
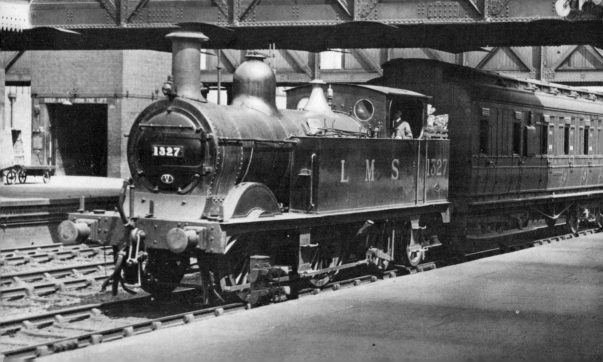

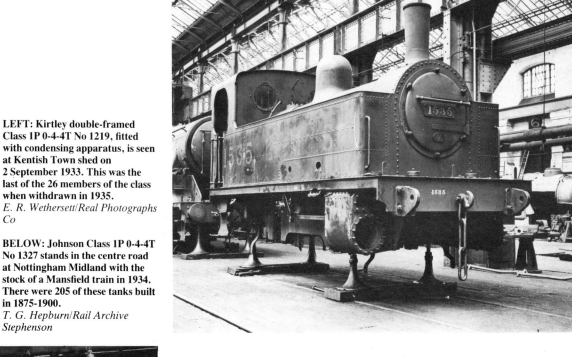

LEFT: Kirtley double-framed Class 1P 0-4-4T No 1219, fitted with condensing apparatus, is seen at Kentish Town shed on 2 September 1933. This was the last of the 26 members of the class when withdrawn in 1935.
E. R. Wethersett/Real Photographs Co

BELOW: Johnson Class 1P 0-4-4T No 1327 stands in the centre road at Nottingham Midland with the stock of a Mansfield train in 1934. There were 205 of these tanks built in 1875-1900.
T. G. Hepburn/Rail Archive Stephenson

TOP: One of the 10 small Deeley 0-4-0Ts No 1535 is seen inside Derby works on 11 July 1937 during overhaul. Introduced in 1907 two of these engines survived to 1966 for shunting at the Staveley Ironworks together with the last five Johnson Class 1F 0-6-0Ts. *L. Hanson*

ABOVE: One of the even smaller Johnson 0-4-0STs built from 1883, No 1516 is fresh from overhaul in Derby works on 29 May 1937.
T. G. Hepburn/Rail Archive Stephenson

London Tilbury & Southend

ABOVE: There were 94 engines of LT&SR origin included in Midland Railway stock at the grouping. Among them were 70 tanks of the Atlantic wheel arrangement. One of these, Thomas Whitelegg Class 2P 4-4-2T No 2175, formerly LTSR No 68 *Mark Lane*, leaves Mill Hill with the 4pm St Pancras-St Albans train on 13 July 1926. This class consisted of 18 engines built in 1900-03 and all but one survived to nationalisation with the last being scrapped in 1953.

UPPER RIGHT: One of the larger T. Whitelegg Class 3P 4-4-2Ts, No 2147, previously LMS No 2176 and LTSR No 79 *Rippleside*, nears Hornchurch with the Ealing-Southend through train in the mid-1930s. The coaches used on this service were the only corridor vehicles owned by the LTSR. The service ceased with the outbreak of World War 2 and was never restored. No 2176, sister to the preserved No 80 *Thundersley*, was one of four built in 1909. They were the final development of Whitelegg's 4-4-2Ts and 12 older engines were rebuilt to the same design. Also a further 35 were built new by the LMS in the years 1923-30.

LOWER RIGHT: One of Robert Whitelegg's Class 3P 4-6-4Ts, No 2104 still in MR livery, waits to leave St Pancras with the 5.25pm St Albans train in 1924. This class totalled eight engines built in 1912, the year the LT&SR was taken over by the Midland. The were all scrapped in 1929-34.
All: F. R. Hebron/Rail Archive Stephenson

North London

ABOVE: William Adams Class 1P 4-4-0T No 2874, allocated LMS No 6435 but never carried, pulls away from signals at Greenwood box in 1924 with the empty stock of a Broad Street-New Barnet train being worked forward to Potters Bar. The four-wheel coaches which form this train were built by the LNWR at Wolverton in 1910 for the Broad Street-Richmond line. Note the bars at the windows — a feature still present on that line. The LNWR took over responsibility for working North London services in 1909 but only a handful of NLR engines were given LNWR numbers at the time, the majority were absorbed into the LNWR stock list in 1923 and carried these until the LMS finally got round to renumbering the few that remained in traffic. Four of these inside-cylinder 4-4-0Ts of 1865-69 survived at the grouping and No 2874, NLR No 109, was the last when withdrawn in 1925.
F. R. Hebron/Rail Archive Stephenson

RIGHT: The well known NLR 0-4-2ST crane engine is seen at Devons Road shed, Bow, in 1926. This engine was originally built as an 0-4-0ST by Sharp Stewart in 1858 for the North & South Western Junction Railway and was rebuilt as a crane engine in 1872. It survived in this form until scrapped in 1951. Bearing No 2896 in the LNWR list it was soon to be given LMS No 7217.
F. R. Hebron/Rail Archive Stephenson

LEFT: One of the 30 Park Class 1F 0-6-0Ts built in 1887-1905, No 7512 is on shed at Devons Road in the late 1920s. The last engine of the class survived until 1960 working on the Cromford & High Peak line in Derbyshire before going to the Bluebell Railway for preservation.
Rail Archive Stephenson

RIGHT: Resplendent in LMS crimson livery, Park Class 1P 4-4-0T No 6444 runs round at Potters Bar after arrival from Broad Street in 1927. The last of these 74 tanks built in 1886-1907, No 6445 was set aside for preservation when withdrawn in 1929 but unfortunately was cut up in 1932.
F. R. Hebron/Rail Archive Stephenson

North Staffordshire

BELOW: Hookham 'F' Class 4P 0-6-4T No 2053 stands in Derby station on a gloomy day in 1930. There were eight of these large tank engines built in 1916-19 and withdrawal came in 1934-36. The fleet of 192 engines of North Staffordshire origin were all withdrawn by the end of 1939.
T. G. Hepburn/Rail Archive Stephenson

RIGHT: One of the six Adams 'L' Class 3F 0-6-2T No 2241 passes through Longport as it nears Stoke-on-Trent with an up goods in the early 1930s. Introduced in 1903 there were eventually 34 engines in this class, the other 28 being known as the 'New L' class which were built in 1908-23. The last loco was withdrawn in 1937 when four were sold to Lancashire Associated Collieries. LMS No 2271 of this batch survives today as NSR No 2.
F. R. Hebron/Rail Archive Stephenson

LEFT: J. H. Adams 'G' Class 3P 4-4-0 No 5410, previously LMS No 595, is seen in May 1928 after having been renumbered to make way for some new Fowler Class 2P 4-4-0s. It is calling at Rudyard with a Macclesfield-Uttoxeter Churnet Valley local formed of LNWR stock shortly before it was withdrawn. There were only four of these 4-4-0s built in 1910.
F. R. Hebron/Rail Archive Stephenson

RIGHT: Longbottom 'D' Class 2F 0-6-0T No 1589 on shed at Stoke-on-Trent, 22 May 1932. This was the most numerous NSR class with 49 built 1882-99.
James R. Clark/Lens of Sutton

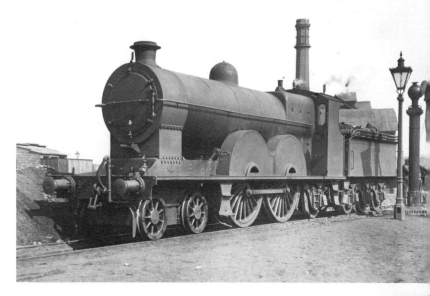

LEFT: With the earliest form of LM&SR initials on its tender, Hughes '8' Class 5P four-cylinder 4-6-0 No 1664 and a sister engine run light outside Crewe station in 1923. It became LMS No 10435.
W. H. Whitworth/Rail Archive Stephenson

BELOW: Hughes 5P 4-6-0 No 10465 passes Oxenholme with a Manchester-Glasgow express in 1929. There were a total of 70 of these engines built in 1921-25.
F. R. Hebron/Rail Archive Stephenson

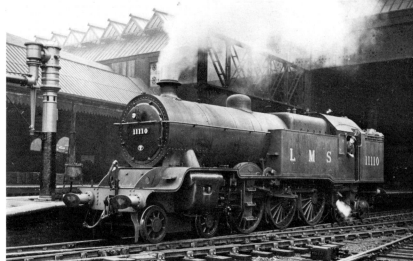

TOP: Aspinall '7' Class 2P 4-4-2 No 10320 of Low Moor shed is seen in the engine siding at Nottingham carriage sidings after arriving on a Bradford-St Pancras express in 1929. There were 40 of these 'Highflyers' built in 1899-1902 and they were scrapped in 1926-34. Note the door in the cab front — an unusual feature of these the only Atlantic tender engines to come into LMS stock.
T. G. Hepburn/Rail Archive Stephenson

ABOVE: Hughes Class 5P 4-6-4T No 11110 runs light out of Manchester Victoria on 8 April 1939. Only 10 of this tank engine version of the Hughes 4-6-0 were built in 1924 and all withdrawn in 1938-42. It was planned to build a further 20 of these large four-cylinder tanks but in the event they were turned out as 4-6-0s Nos 10455-74. *John P. Wilson*

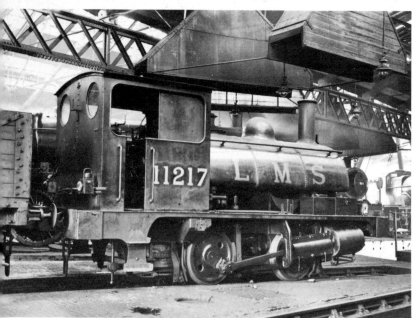

LEFT: Aspinall 'Pug' Class '21' 0-4-0ST No 11217 inside Derby roundhouse on 16 October 1938. The 'Pugs' were the smallest engines among the 1,721 of LYR design taken into LMS stock and were built in 1891-1910.
L. Hanson

RIGHT: Aspinall '27' Class 2F 0-6-0 No 12117 awaiting duty at Manchester Victoria on 4 April 1939. This class was the most numerous on the LYR with 448 built in 1889-1917.
John P. Wilson

LEFT: Aspinall '5' Class 2P 2-4-2T No 10732 leaves Moston with a Manchester-Bury train c1925. There were 309 of these versatile radial tanks constructed in 1889-1910.
G. W. Smith/Neville Fields Collection

RIGHT: Barton Wright Class 1P 4-4-0 No 10106 at Preston in the late 1920s. The 30 engines in this class were built in 1888-89 and No 10106 was one of three rebuilt by Hughes in 1910-15 with a Belpaire firebox and extended smokebox.
W. H. Whitworth/Rail Archive Stephenson

BELOW: Hughes '28' Class 3F 0-6-0 No 12574 heads a Sowerby Bridge-Todmorden local away from Mytholmroyd on 8 August 1947. This one of 63 engines rebuilt from Aspinall '27' class engines in 1913-22 and 20 were built new in 1912. *E. R. Wethersett/Real Photographs Co*

UPPER RIGHT: Hughes '31' Class 7F 0-8-0 No 12857 steams over Luddendenfoot water troughs with an eastbound freight on the Calder Valley line, 7 September 1945. This class introduced in 1912 eventually totalled 150 engines, several having been rebuilt from Aspinall and Hughes '30' class. *E. R. Wethersett/Real Photographs Co*

LOWER RIGHT: One of the earlier Hughes 0-8-0s, '30' Class 6F No 12834 awaits its next turn of duty inside Wigan Wallgate shed on 2 May 1948. Appropriately nicknamed 'Teddy Bears' there were 69 in the class introduced in 1910, 29 had been rebuilt from Aspinall '30' class, and together with the '31' class became extinct in 1951. How we would like to see a set of 'Daily Engine Arrangements' such as must have been set out on the board to the left again! *J. G. Dewing*

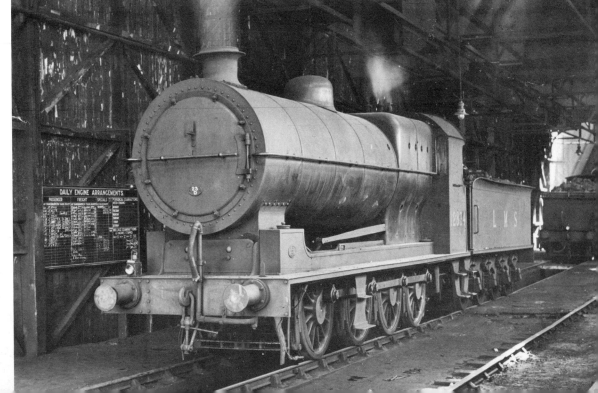

Furness

BELOW: Pettigrew Class 2F 0-6-0 No 12471 pulls slowly out of the yard at Carnforth with a goods train for Barrow-in-Furness in May 1928. There were 16 engines included in this class, 12 having 4ft 8in diameter driving wheels and the remaining four 5ft 1in. They were all built in 1899-1907 and had all been withdrawn by the end of 1936.

UPPER RIGHT: One of the four Pettigrew Class 1P 6ft 6in 4-4-0s built in 1900-1, No 10144 departs from Carlisle Citadel with a Maryport train in 1929. They were scrapped between 1934 and 1940.

LOWER RIGHT: Largest among the 136 Furness locomotives inherited by the LMS were the five Rutherford 4-6-4Ts designed and built by Kitsons in 1920. No 11104 passes Hest Bank with a Barrow-in-Furness-Lancaster train in 1927. Withdrawal came in 1934-40.
All: F. R. Hebron/Rail Archive Stephenson

51

Glasgow & South Western

ABOVE: Peter Drummond '51' Class 4F 2-6-0 No 17829 heads a Carlisle-Glasgow via Dumfries Class 'H' goods near Rockcliffe just south of the border in the summer of 1936. One of 11 Moguls built in 1915, No 17829 was the last surviving G&SWR tender engine when withdrawn in 1947. The 527 engines to come into LMS ownership from this railway were mostly withdrawn quite quickly with only one other class surviving after 1937. *E. E. Smith*

UPPER RIGHT: Manson '495' Class 3P 4-6-0 No 14671 waits in Glasgow St Enoch on 16 July 1926. There were two varieties of Manson 4-6-0, 17 of this type built in 1903-11 and two of the '512' Class 3P engines built in 1911. All had gone by the end of 1934. *T. G. Hepburn/Rail Archive Stephenson*

LOWER RIGHT: One of the six R. H. Whitelegg '540' Class 5P 4-6-4Ts built in 1922, No 15404 is seen being coaled in the early 1930s. They were all scrapped in 1934-35. *Lens of Sutton*

**BELOW: Smellie Class 1P 4-4-0
No 14116 leaves Glasgow St Enoch
with a stopping train c1929. Built
in 1882 it was the first of a class of
22 engines, 13 of which were later
rebuilt with larger domed boilers
(see opposite).**
James R. Clark/Lens of Sutton

LEFT: One of the 13 Smellie 6ft 1¼in 4-4-0s rebuilt with a larger domed boiler, Class 2P No 14118 stands in a centre road at Glasgow St Enoch decked out in the finery of the pre-1928 LMS crimson lake in 1926. The class became extinct in 1934.
T. G. Hepburn/Rail Archive Stephenson

RIGHT: Manson Class 1P 6ft 9in 4-4-0 No 14199 reverses out of Glasgow St Enoch after arrival with a stopping train on 16 July 1926. Built 1892-1904 the last of these engines went in 1933 swept aside by the Fowler 2P 4-4-0s.
T. G. Hepburn/Rail Archive Stephenson

LOWER LEFT: One of the Manson 6ft 9in 4-4-0s rebuilt with a larger boiler to Class 2P, No 14170 enters Glasgow St Enoch with a stopping train c1929.
James R. Clark/Lens of Sutton

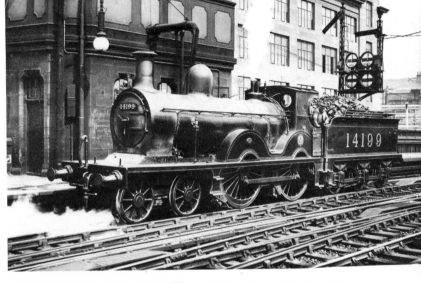

LEFT: Manson '115' Class 3F 0-6-0 No 17483 stands in Glasgow St Enoch carrying express passenger headcode on 16 July 1926. This photograph shows the pre-1928 freight engine livery to good effect. It was one of 23 engines fitted with larger boilers out of a class of 36 built in 1900-10.
T. G. Hepburn/Rail Archive Stephenson

Caledonian

ABOVE: The one time pride of the Caley, McIntosh '903' Class 4P 4-6-0 No 14752, formerly named *Cardean*, departs from Perth General with a Glasgow train shortly before withdrawal in 1930. There were originally five engines in the '903' class built in 1906 but one was written off in the Quintinshill accident in 1915. *T. G. Hepburn/Rail Archive Stephenson*

UPPER RIGHT: Pickersgill '60' Class 3P 4-6-0 No 14633, one of 20 built by the LMS in 1925-26, enters Stirling with a northbound troop train formed entirely of LNWR stock on 14 July 1938. There were only six of these engines built by the CR in 1916-17. *John P. Wilson*

LOWER RIGHT: The last 4-6-0 type designed for the CR was Pickersgill's '191' Class 3P of which eight were built in 1922 for the Oban line. No 14622 stands in Stirling station with an Oban-Glasgow train c1926. Built by NBL, they were scrapped during the war years with the last going in 1945. *T. G. Hepburn/Rail Archive Stephenson*

LEFT: McIntosh 'Dunalastair IV' Class 2P 4-4-0 No 14351 passes the ticket platform as it leaves Perth with an Aberdeen-Glasgow Buchanan Street train c1930. These were the final development of the saturated 'Dunalastair' 4-4-0s first introduced in 1896. There were 19 of these later engines turned out from 1904. *T. G. Hepburn/Rail Archive Stephenson*

BELOW: 'Dunalastair II' Class 2P 4-4-0 No 14335, formerly named *Breadalbane*, waits to leave Motherwell with a stopping train for Glasgow Central on 2 August 1938. The 15 engines of this series were all built in 1897. *L. Hanson*

ABOVE: A pair of 'Dunalastair III' Class 2P 4-4-0s with No 14348 leading, prepare to leave Callander with a special train for Dunblane in 1936. *E. E. Smith*

RIGHT: McIntosh '139' Class 3P 4-4-0 No 14447, still with its smokebox wing plates, pilots a Pickersgill Class 3P 4-4-0 out of Aberdeen with a Glasgow express in the mid-1920s.
LPC/Real Photographs Co

LEFT: Unique among the 1,107 engines (including 30 built by the LMS) of Caledonian design was the famous CR single No 123 built as an exhibition engine by Neilson & Co in 1886. It is seen here as LMS No 14010 on Perth shed, 16 June 1931. It was withdrawn in 1935 and restored to CR livery as No 123 and survives in the Glasgow Museum of Transport.
James R. Clark/Lens of Sutton

BELOW: Dugald Drummond 'Jumbo' Class 2F 0-6-0 No 17404 passes through Gretna with a southbound loose-coupled goods in 1930. The Drummond 'Jumbos' were numerically the largest class on the CR with 244 examples built in 1883-97. All came into LMS ownership and all but six passed to BR in 1948.
F. R. Hebron/Rail Archive Stephenson

TOP: McIntosh '812' Class 3F 0-6-0 No 17572 heads out of Perth with a southbound mixed freight c1930. The first three vans are of LNWR origin while the other three are LYR, LMS and MR respectively. The '812' class 0-6-0s were introduced in 1899 and a total of 96 were built in 10 years.

ABOVE: One of the five McIntosh '34' Class 3F 2-6-0s, No 17800 on Kingmoor shed, Carlisle, in the mid 1930s. They were built in 1912. *Both: T. G. Hepburn/Rail Archive Stephenson*

RIGHT: Lambie Class 1P 4-4-0T No 15025 runs round at Connel Ferry in spring 1937 when it was the Ballachulish branch engine. Originally built for working the Glasgow Central underground line in 1893, there were 12 in this class which became extinct in 1938. *E. E. Smith*

UPPER RIGHT: Class 2P 0-4-4T No 15233 nears Killin Junction with the one coach Killin branch train in Spring 1937. This was the final version of the McIntosh 0-4-4T first introduced in 1895 and was from a batch of 14 built by Pickersgill in 1915-22. The LMS built 10 further engines in 1925 bringing the total to 136. *E. E. Smith*

LOWER RIGHT: The last surviving Dugald Drummond Class 1P 0-4-4T No 15103 approaches Wick with the 2.40pm mixed train from Lybster on 22 August 1935. One of 24 built in 1884-91 it survived until the Lybster branch closed in 1944. *K. A. C. R. Nunn/LCGB Ken Nunn Collection*

ABOVE: One of the LMS built Class 2P 0-4-4Ts, No 15266 makes a surprising sight at Nottingham Midland after arrival with a train from Mansfield on 20 June 1934.

RIGHT: McIntosh Class 2F No 16173, the final engine built of 23 in 1911-21 which lasted until 1958-62. *Both: T. G. Hepburn/Rail Archive Stephenson*

LEFT: Jones 'Loch' Class 2P 4-4-0 No 14384 *Loch Laggan* pilots a 'Castle' class 4-6-0 out of Blair Atholl for the 16-mile climb to Druimauchdar summit with a Glasgow-Inverness train c1930.
T. G. Hepburn/Rail Archive Stephenson

BELOW: 'Jones Goods' Class 4F 4-6-0 No 17919 brings an Inverness goods through Muir of Ord c1930. There were 15 of these, Britain's first 4-6-0s, built in 1894.
Lens of Sutton

Highland

ABOVE: There were 15 Jones 'Loch' class 4-4-0s built in 1896 and a further three in 1917. In early LMS days 10 were rebuilt with larger boilers of Caledonian origin. One of these, No 14392 *Loch Naver* **leaves Hermitage Tunnel near Dunkeld with a Perth-Blair Atholl local c1930. Two of these rebuilds survived to come into BR ownership and the last to be withdrawn was** *Loch Tay* **in 1950.**
F. R. Hebron/Rail Archive Stephenson

LEFT: 'Jones Goods' 4-6-0
No 17929, with a plain chimney
and no wing plates, stands on
Inverness turntable in the spring of
1936 complete with a small wooden
snowplough. *E. E. Smith*

BELOW: Peter Drummond
'Castle' Class 3P 4-6-0 No 14684
Duncraig Castle climbs the 1 in 60
to Slochd summit with an
Inverness-Perth stopping train in
1937. A total of 19 'Castles' were
built in 1900-17 and were of two
varieties.
*F. R. Hebron/Rail Archive
Stephenson*

ABOVE: Cumming 'Clan'
Class 4P 4-6-0 No 14763 *Clan
Fraser* at Callander with an
evening Glasgow-Oban express on
31 August 1938. Allocated to
St Rollox this was one of several
'Clans' exiled from the Highland
by the Stanier 'Black Fives'. Eight
examples were built in 1919-21.
*T. G. Hepburn/Rail Archive
Stephenson*

RIGHT: Drummond Class 3F
0-6-0 No 17698 shunts a train of
cattle trucks at Grantown-on-Spey
in April 1938. Known as the
'Barney' class, a dozen were built
in 1900-7 and were the only 0-6-0
tender engines on the HR.
Gavin L. Wilson

ABOVE: One of the six fated Smith 'River' Class 4P 4-6-0s built in 1915, No 14759 heads an Inverness-Perth train near Killiekrankie in the early 1930s. When first built the HR refused to take delivery of them as they were considered too heavy for the line and were sold to the Caledonian only to run on the Highland line in LMS days. *F. R. Hebron/Rail Archive Stephenson*

BELOW: An unidentified Cumming 'Clan Goods' Class 5F 4-6-0 pilots a Drummond 'Small Ben' class 4-4-0 out of Kyle of Lochalsh with an Inverness train in 1937. There were eight of these mixed traffic engines built in 1918-19, thus preceding by one year the 'Clan' 4-6-0s from which they derived their name. The last was withdrawn in 1952.
F. R. Hebron/Rail Archive Stephenson

RIGHT: Peter Drummond 'Small Ben' Class 2P 4-4-0 No 14413 *Ben Alligan* at Blair Atholl in the early 1930s. Built in 1898-1906 there were 20 'Small Bens' and No 14398 *Ben Alder* survived to be the last Highland engine when withdrawn in 1953. It was retained with a view to preservation but was eventually broken up.
T. G. Hepburn/Rail Archive Stephenson

ABOVE: The last surviving Peter Drummond 'Large Ben' Class 2P 4-4-0 No 14422 *Ben a'Chaoruinn* at Elgin with a Keith-Forres train in 1936, a year before it was withdrawn. Only six engines of this design were built in 1908-09.
F. R. Hebron/Rail Archive Stephenson

RIGHT: One of the eight Peter Drummond Class 4P 0-6-4Ts built in 1909-11 for banking duties, No 15307 is seen at Blair Atholl c1930.
T. G. Hepburn/Rail Archive Stephenson

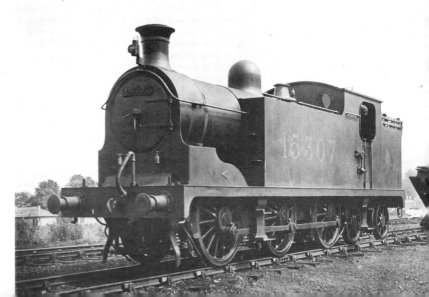

Standard LMS Engines

ABOVE: In 1924 during George Hughes short spell as CME of the LMS the decision was taken to adopt the MR Johnson Class 1, later '3F' 0-6-0T of 1899 as rebuilt by Fowler as the standard LMS shunting engine. A total of 422, including seven built for the S&DJR were built up to 1931. No 16585 is seen departing from Potters Bar with a Broad Street train formed of ancient NLR four-wheel coaches in 1929. It was later renumbered 7502.

UPPER RIGHT: Two further MR designs chosen for further construction were the Fowler Class 2P 4-4-0 and the three-cylinder Class 4P compound, both with 6ft 9in driving wheels. A total of 135 '2Ps' were built in 1928-32 and 195 compounds were turned out in 1924-32. Here Class 2P No 619 pilots Class 4P compound No 1144 at Gretna with the 5.10pm Carlisle-Dumfries express in 1930. Three further '2Ps' were built for the S&DJR in 1928.

LOWER RIGHT: The Fowler Class 4F 0-6-0 was also chosen as an LMS standard engine and no less than 575 being built in 1924-41 which together with the 192 MR engines and five taken over from the S&DJR gave a class total of 772. No 4418 crosses the West Lynn viaduct over the Great Ouse with an excursion for Great Yarmouth on the M&GN in the early 1930s.
All: F. R. Hebron/Rail Archive Stephenson

BELOW: The first truly new design to appear on the LMS was the Class 4F 2-6-0 in 1926. Known at first as the Horwich Moguls they were designed by George Hughes but did not appear until after his retirement and had several Fowler fittings not least of which was the narrow tender. No 13004, in crimson livery, departs from York with an excursion returning from Scarborough formed of LYR non-corridor coaches in the late 1920s.
LPC/Real Photographs Co

BOTTOM LEFT: Horwich Mogul No 2919, formerly No 13219, climbs Grayrigg bank with a down Class H goods train in 1935. These capable engines became affectionately known as 'Crabs' because of the raised running plate over the cylinders. Their power classification was increased from '4F' to '5P4F', then to '5P5F' and during World War 2 they became '5F'. In BR days they were '5MT' and '6P5F' for a short time.
F. R. Hebron/Rail Archive Stephenson

BELOW: The 'Crabs' were favourite engines for hauling summer Saturday relief express and excursion trains. Derby based No 13098 is seen threading the beautiful Derbyshire landscape near Whatstandwell with an up excursion formed of Bain MR low roof suburban coaches in the early 1930s. A total of 245 'Crabs' were built and they were at first numbered 13000-244 but they were renumbered 2700-2944 from 1934.
LPC/Real Photographs Co

LEFT: 'Crab' 2-6-0 No 13026, in crimson livery, approaches Oxenholme with an up goods in May 1928.

BELOW: No 13180 tackles the almost 10-mile climb from Beattock to the summit with a down freight in the early 1930s. Rear end assistance is being provided by a Caley 0-4-4T.
Both: F. R. Hebron/Rail Archive Stephenson

ABOVE: No 13180 is seen again, now numbered 2880, having just crossed the Ligg viaduct on the 1 in 69/73 gradient between Pinwherry and Barrhill with a Glasgow St Enoch-Stranraer train in 1936.

RIGHT: Five 'Crabs' were fitted with Lentz rotary-cam poppet valve gear in 1931 and No 13125 so fitted is seen near Hornchurch in 1935 with a St Pancras-Southend train. In 1953 these five engines had their Lentz gear replaced by Reidinger poppet valve gear.
Both: F. R. Hebron/Rail Archive Stephenson

BELOW: Fowler Class 4P 2-6-4T No 2403 departs from Birmingham New Street with a semi-fast train for Stafford on 7 May 1938. The first of the 125 engines of this class appeared in 1927 but No 2403 is from the final 30 which were fitted with side window cabs with full height doors. *L. Hanson*

UPPER RIGHT: A Melton Mowbray-Nottingham local coasts downgrade from Edwalton behind Class 4P 2-6-4T No 2340 on 7 July 1934. An LYR compartment third is next to the engine while the rest of the train is formed of Bain MR low roof compartment stock.
T. G. Hepburn/Rail Archive Stephenson

LOWER RIGHT: Another of the side window cab Fowler 2-6-4Ts, No 2398 leaves New Mills (LNWR) with a Manchester London Road-Buxton train on 5 June 1937. The first and third carriages are of the final LMS style of steel panelled compartment stock while the second is of the previous style.
R. D. Pollard/Neville Fields Collection

ABOVE: In 1927 the first three 2-6-0+0-6-2T Beyer-Garratt locomotives entered service followed by a further 30 in 1930. One of the latter engines, No 4980 gets moving out of Toton yard past Long Eaton station with a coal train for Brent on 27 August 1932.
T. G. Hepburn/Rail Archive Stephenson

BELOW: The two batches of Beyer-Garratts were originally numbered 4967-96 and 4997-99 and were renumbered 7967-99 in 1938. No 7971 accelerates a down goods through Kettering in June 1939. All were fitted with rotary coal bunkers except two of the original engines, Nos 4998-9. *C. R. L. Coles*

BELOW: Another notable LMS design to appear in 1927 was the 'Royal Scot' Class 6P three-cylinder 4-6-0. They were designed and built by the North British Locomotive Co in close collaboration with Derby and 50 engines were delivered within twelve months of the order having been placed. Nos 6100-24 were given the names of British Army Regiments while Nos 6125-49 revived the names carried by historic locomotives. Unfortunately these names were later removed in favour of more regiments though some did reappear on Stanier 'Jubilee' class 4-6-0s and a lone 'Patriot'. No 6109 *Royal Engineer* climbs Madeley bank away from Crewe with an afternoon Liverpool-Euston express in May 1928. A further 20 'Royal Scots' were built at Derby in 1930.
F. R. Hebron/Rail Archive Stephenson

ABOVE: Fowler 'Royal Scot' Class 6P 4-6-0 No 6135 *Samson* climbs Shap with the down 10am 'Royal Scot' from Euston to Glasgow c1930.
LPC/Real Photographs Co

BELOW: Resplendent in its original 1927 livery, No 6139 *Ajax* passes Bushey & Oxhey station with the down 'Royal Scot' in 1929.
F. R. Hebron/Rail Archive Stephenson

RIGHT: 'Royal Scot' No 6144 *Honourable Artillery Company,* **formerly** *Ostrich,* **approaches Euston with an up express in 1935.** *J. G. Dewing*

BELOW: The experimental high-pressure Class 6 three-cylinder compound 4-6-0 No 6399 *Fury* **languishes inside Derby paint shop awaiting a decision on its future. Built in 1930 this engine suffered many problems not least of which was a fatal burst high-pressure tube. Stanier rebuilt it in 1935, the first of his taper boiler rebuilds as No 6170** *British Legion.*
W. H. Whitworth/Rail Archive Stephenson

LEFT: 'Royal Scot' No 6124 *London Scottish* passes through the castle wall as it passes Conway with the up 'Irish Mail' from Holyhead to Euston in the early 1930s. It is fitted with the first type of straight smoke deflectors fitted to the class after a 'Royal Scot' was involved in an accident believed due to the driver's vision being obscured by drifting smoke. *LPC/Real Photographs Co*

RIGHT: The straight deflectors soon gave way to those with angled tops as on No 6151 *The Royal Horse Guardsman* waiting at Carlisle. A Fowler Class 2P 4-4-0 No 605 is on the right with a Dumfries train in 1936. *E. E. Smith*

ABOVE: Fowler Class 7F 0-8-0 No 9634 heads west over Luddendenfoot water troughs with a coal train on the Calder Valley main line, 7 September 1945. These engines earned themselves the nickname of 'Austin Sevens'.
E. R. Wethersett/Real Photographs Co

BELOW: An 'Austin Seven', No 9504, is seen in full cry attacking the 1 in 200 gradient out of Nottingham to Edwalton with a Toton-Brent coal train on 7 July 1934. Introduced in 1929 a total of 175 of this class were built.
T. G. Hepburn/Rail Archive Stephenson

LEFT: Fowler Class 3P 2-6-2T No 2 at Crewe in the 1930s. The 70 engines of this class, first introduced in 1930, were originally numbered 15500-69 and were renumbered 1-70 from 1934.
T. G. Hepburn/Rail Archive Stephenson

RIGHT: Push and pull fitted No 20 waits to leave Stanmore with the branch auto train for Harrow & Wealdstone in the mid-1930s.
C. R. L. Coles

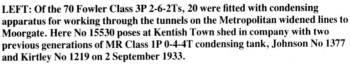

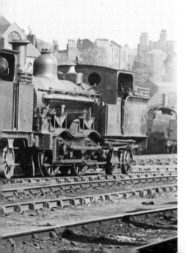

LEFT: Of the 70 Fowler Class 3P 2-6-2Ts, 20 were fitted with condensing apparatus for working through the tunnels on the Metropolitan widened lines to Moorgate. Here No 15530 poses at Kentish Town shed in company with two previous generations of MR Class 1P 0-4-4T condensing tank, Johnson No 1377 and Kirtley No 1219 on 2 September 1933.
T. G. Hepburn/Rail Archive Stephenson

ABOVE: No 16 banks a northbound freight up Shap in 1950. There were two of these engines shedded at Tebay at this time for banking duties. *E. E. Smith*

LEFT: Following on from the rebuilding of the LNWR 'Claughton' engines with larger boilers Derby rebuilt two in 1930 with the same large boiler but with a completely new three-cylinder chassis based on that of the 'Royal Scots'. The first of the three-cylinder 'Claughton' rebuilds, Class 5XP No 5971 departs from Carlisle with the up 'Thames Clyde Express' in 1931. These engines were at first nicknamed 'Baby Scots' but when the name *Patriot* was transferred in 1937 from a withdrawn 'Claughton' to No 5971 they officially became known as the 'Patriot' class. The first two rebuilds retained the large centred driving wheels and other parts from the engines they replaced. *F. R. Hebron/Rail Archive Stephenson*

BELOW: The second 'Patriot', No 5902 *Sir Frank Ree*, by now fitted with straight smoke deflectors, stands in the centre road at Nottingham Midland in 1932. From 1933 a further 50 more were built of which all but the last 10 were nominally regarded as rebuilds and carried the numbers of the engines they had replaced. *J. N. Hall/Rail Archive Stephenson*

BELOW: 'Patriot' No 6011 comes down the bank from Edwalton towards Nottingham with a St Pancras-Leeds express in 1934. The empty milk tanks are bound for Appleby.

BOTTOM: No 5971, latter to be named *Croxteth* and then *Patriot*, climbs away from Nottingham towards Edwalton with the 1.34pm express for St Pancras on 18 June 1932. *Both: T. G. Hepburn/Rail Archive Stephenson*

ABOVE: One of the beautifully turned out Bushbury 'Patriots' No 5526 yet to be named *Morecambe and Heysham*, passes Hillmorton with a Birmingham-Euston two-hour express in 1935. *F. R. Hebron/Rail Archive Stephenson*

BELOW: 'Patriot' 4-6-0 No 5933, which was later to become No 5521 *Rhyl*, is seen taking water at Kentish Town shed, at this time its home depot on **2 September 1933**. *E. R. Wethersett/Real Photographs Co*

UPPER LEFT: From 1934 the 'Patriots' were renumbered 5500-41 with the 10 engines built that year following on. No 5537 *Private E. Sykes, V.C.* departs from Manchester London Road with the 12.05pm 'Lancastrian' for Euston on 1 June 1936. *R. D. Pollard/Neville fields Collection*

LOWER LEFT: Another of the well kept Bushbury 'Patriots', No 5521 *Rhyl* waits to leave Birmingham New Street with an express for Manchester on 7 May 1938. *L. Hanson*

BELOW: Class 2P 0-4-4T No 6409 nears Brickett Wood with the 7.38pm Watford-St Albans train on 13 June 1937. The 10 members of this class appeared in 1932 after William Stanier had taken over as CME of the LMS. However it is obvious that the design dates from the Fowler era. *K. A. C. R. Numm/LCGB Ken Nunn Collection*

BOTTOM: No 6401 is seen on arrival at Nottingham Midland with a train from Derby in 1933 that is to form the stock of an express to St Pancras. Note the Reid MR 12-wheel dining car. *T. G. Hepburn/Rail Archive Stephenson*

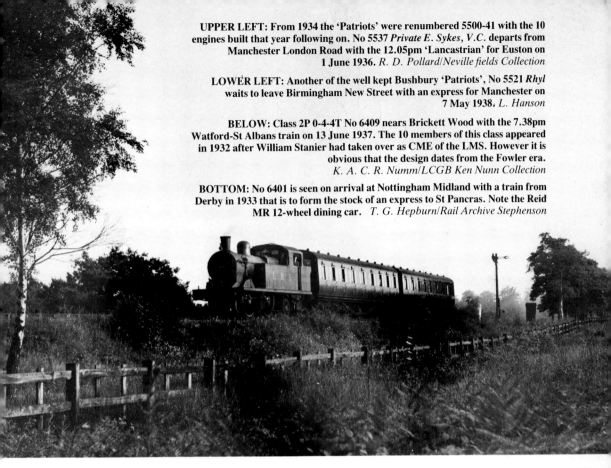

UPPER LEFT: The first Stanier locomotive to enter service was 'Princess Royal' Class 7P four-cylinder Pacific No 6200 *The Princess Royal* which emerged from the erecting shops at Crewe in June 1933. *The Princess Royal*, allocated to Camden and carrying a Caledonian route indicator, heads the up 'Royal Scot' south of Tring in 1934. The first two 'Princess Royals' were coupled with new tenders of distinctively Midland appearance.
F. R. Hebron/Rail Archive Stephenson

LEFT: Two years later *The Princess Royal* roars north over Bushey water troughs with the down 'Merseyside Express' from Euston to Liverpool Lime Street on 20 June 1936. No 6200 has now acquired a Stanier tender of 9 tons coal and 4,000 gallons water capacity. The second coach is one of five first class lounge brakes built at Derby in 1928 and regularly used in this train.
E. R. Wethersett/Real Photographs Co

ABOVE: A postwar view of No 6200 *The Princess Royal*, now allocated to Edge Hill, taking water from Bushey troughs with the 10.30am Euston-Liverpool express in 1947. The engine now has a domed boiler and has the final 10 ton, 4,000 gallon tender allocated to the class.
F. R. Hebron/Rail Archive Stephenson

LEFT: In 1935 there came out what might have been the third 'Princess Royal' Pacific but which was the unique Stanier/Metropolitan-Vickers turbine locomotive No 6202. The 'Turbomotive' as it became known is seen after arrival at Euston with an express from Liverpool c1937. *J. N. Hall/Rail Archive Stephenson*

LEFT: The second 'Princess Royal' appeared later in 1933 followed by a further 10 in 1935. The final member of the class, No 6212 *Duchess of Kent*, is seen heading north towards Tring with the 1.35pm Euston-Aberdeen express on 23 August 1938.
E. R. Wethersett/Real Photographs Co

RIGHT: Another view of No 6212 *Duchess of Kent*, showing the smokebox door secured by Derby type lugs, seen sweeping through Elvanfoot with the southbound 'Midday Scot' in 1936.
F. R. Hebron/Rail Archive Stephenson

BELOW: No 6208 *Princess Helena Victoria* waits at Rugby with the down 'Royal Scot' c1936.
T. G. Hepburn/Rail Archive Stephenson

BELOW: 'Princess Royal' class Pacific No 6203 *Princess Margaret Rose* leaves Northchurch Tunnel south of Tring with a Euston-Liverpool express on 17 June 1947.
E. R. Wethersett/Real Photographs Co

ABOVE: The second Stanier engine to emerge from Crewe works in 1933 was Class 4F 2-6-0 No 13245 seen here on shed at Crewe South, 7 April 1934. Note the top feed and safety valves combined in GWR style.
T. G. Hepburn/Rail Archive Stephenson

BELOW: The 40 engines of this class built in 1933-34 were at first numbered 13245-84 but were renumbered 2945-84 from 1934. No 2971 with conventionally placed safety valves is seen in the mid 1930s.
T. G. Hepburn/Rail Archive Stephenson

ABOVE: In 1934 the first of the 191 Stanier 'Jubilee' or Class 5XP three-cylinder 4-6-0s began to appear. No 5593, later named *Kolhapur*, is seen climbing away from Oxenholme with a down milk train in 1935.   *F. R. Hebron/Rail Archive Stephenson*

UPPER RIGHT: On the Midland line No 5656 *Cochrane*, fitted with a domed boiler, leaves Elstree Tunnel with the 2.35pm St Pancras-Manchester Central express on 5 June 1937.
E. R. Wethersett/Real Photographs Co

LOWER RIGHT: In 1935 'Jubilee' 4-6-0 No 5642 exchanged identities with the first member of the class and was specially turned out in a gloss black livery with all the brightwork, top feed cover, steam pipes and raised numbers chrome plated. At the same time the engine was named *Silver Jubilee* in honour of King George V's Silver Jubilee. No 5552 *Silver Jubilee* is seen at Nottingham Midland while making a tour of the LMS system in 1935.   *T. G. Hepburn/Rail Archive Stephenson*

ABOVE: 'Jubilee' Class 5XP 4-6-0 No 5574, later named *India*, nears Rugby at Hillmorton with a Euston-Manchester London Road express in 1935. The line from Northampton can be seen on the left.
F. R. Hebron/Rail Archive Stephenson

BELOW: A heavy empty passenger train heads east over the Calder Valley main line towards Mytholmroyd behind 'Jubilee' No 5710 *Irresistible*, coupled with a Fowler tender, on 18 August 1947. *E. R. Wethersett/Real Photographs Co*

ABOVE: In 1934 Stanier's three-cylinder taper boiler version of the Fowler Class 4P 2-6-4T was introduced, primarily for use on the LT&SR line from Fenchurch Street. No 2504 leaves Watford Tunnel on the slow lines with a Euston-Bletchley stopping train on 5 August 1935. The 37 engines of this class were all built at Derby in 1934, the first 24 having cab doors in the style of the final batch of Fowler 2-6-4Ts. *E. R. Wethersett/Real Photographs Co*

UPPER RIGHT: A sight of one of the Stanier three-cylinder 2-6-4Ts on the line for which they were intended. No 2534 approaches Southend bunker first with a stopping train from Fenchurch Street via Upminster on 17 August 1936. This shows the latter style of cab door.
E. R. Wethersett/Real Photographs Co

LOWER RIGHT: The first of the Stanier Class 4P two-cylinder 2-6-4Ts built in 1935, No 2537 is seen on Crewe South shed when still quite new c1936. All the three-cylinder engines and the first eight two-cylinder engines had domeless boilers.
T. G. Hepburn/Rail Archive Stephenson

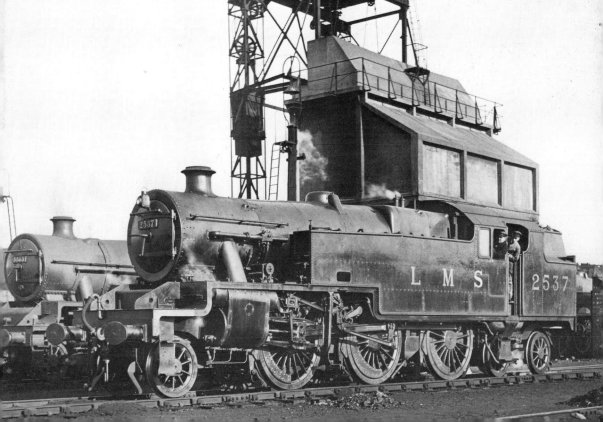

BELOW: Stanier Class 4P 2-6-4T No 2553 enters Nottingham Midland with the empty stock for a Derby train in the late 1930s. This was one of 73 engines of this class built by the North British Locomotive Company in 1936-37 all the remainder out of a class total of 206 were built at Derby. *T. G. Hepburn/Rail Archive Stephenson*

BELOW: Stanier Class 5P5F 4-6-0 No 5032, allocated to Gloucester, climbs the Lickey Incline with a Bristol Temple Meads-Birmingham New Street train in 1935. No 5032 was from the first batch of the ubiquitous 'Black Fives' built by the Vulcan Foundry in 1934-35 and differs from the first batch of Crewe built engines in that the pipes to the top feed are not recessed into the boiler lagging and there is no step plate under the smokebox door, both features were later modified to conform with the Crewe built engines. *F. R. Hebron/Rail Archive Stephenson*

UPPER RIGHT: From the first batch of Crewe built 'Black Fives', No 5011 takes water at Tain while working the late afternoon Inverness-Wick trains c1936. *C. R. Gordon/Lens of Sutton*

LOWER RIGHT: No 5165 at Stirling with a Perth-Glasgow train on 30 August 1938. Note the former Caledonian Pullman car next to the loco, one of 16 sold to the LMS in 1933. This engine is from the batch of 100 'Black Fives' built by Armstrong Whitworth in 1935.
T. G. Hepburn/Rail Archive Stephenson

UPPER LEFT: 'Black Five' No 5040, now fitted with a domed boiler but retaining the taller chimney of the earlier engines, passes Sheet Stores Junction with a Nottingham-Derby stopping train on 4 June 1938. *John P. Wilson*

LOWER LEFT: Brand new No 5175 stands in Nottingham Midland station in 1935. Engines from No 5225 were built with domed boilers. *T. G. Hepburn/Rail Archive Stephenson*

TOP: One of the later Armstrong Whitworth 'Black Fives' No 5379, painted in the short lived 1936 livery and 'Jubilee' class 4-6-0 No 5595 *Southern Rhodesia* photographed at the south end of Crewe Station c1939. *T. G. Hepburn/Rail Archive Stephenson*

ABOVE: No 5325 heads a down freight beside the Oxford Canal near Brinklow on 16 September 1937. This class continued to be constructed with various modifications and experimental versions until 1951 when 842 had been built. *T. G. Hepburn/Rail Archive Stephenson*

ABOVE: Stanier Class 3P 2-6-2T
No 155 makes a pleasing sight as it
accelerates away from Potters Bar
with a Broad Street train on
13 May 1939. The low roof Bain
MR compartment stock was a
great improvement over the
antiquated NLR four-wheelers and
its comfort doubtless surpassed
that of the Gresley articulated
stock the LNER used on GN
suburban services. *J. G. Dewing*

RIGHT: One of the six Class 3P
2-6-2Ts fitted with larger boilers,
No 163 stands in Nottingham
Midland Station on 7 August 1948.
*T. G. Hepburn/Rail Archive
Stephenson*

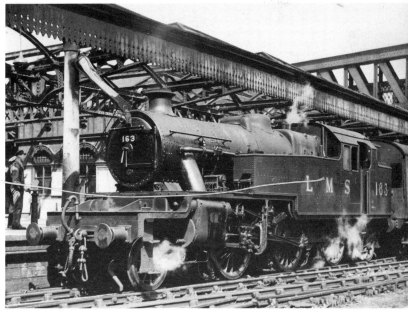

LEFT: It is not always appreciated that the Class 8F 2-8-0s were numerically the largest class of Stanier engines with 852 constructed between 1935 and 1946. This is because only 666 eventually came into BR stock. Many of the '8Fs' were built for War Department use during World War 2 and others were requisitioned from the LMS for war service. Many of these engines were never to return, either being written off during hostilities or were taken into stock on a Middle Eastern railway. At the time of writing in 1985 a few '8Fs' survive in Turkey. No 8069 climbs away from Nottingham on the Melton Mowbray line with a Toton-Brent coal train, 4 June 1938.
T. G. Hepburn/Rail Archive Stephenson

BELOW: Stanier '8Fs' were built by the other three major railway companies in Britain in 1943-46 and Swindon built No 8460 leans to the curve at Mytholmroyd soon after taking water from Luddendenfoot troughs with a westbound coal train on 18 August 1947.
E. R. Wethersett/Real Photographs Co

ABOVE: Stanier 'Coronation' Class 7P 4-6-2 No 6222 *Queen Mary* **climbs Shap with the down 'Coronation Scot' on 27 August 1937. There were five 'Coronation' Pacifics built in 1937 painted in a blue and silver livery for working the 'Coronation Scot' between Euston and Glasgow.**
James R. Clark/Lens of Sutton

UPPER RIGHT: The first 'Coronation' Pacific, No 6220 *Coronation* **itself is towed into Euston on 24 June 1937 for exhibition prior to the trial run of the 'Coronation Scot' five days later.**
E. R. Wethersett/Rail Archive Stephenson

LOWER RIGHT: A striking rear view of No 6223 *Princess Alice* **departing from Euston with the down 'Coronation Scot' on 16 July 1937.** *John P. Wilson*

UPPER LEFT: In 1938 10 Stanier 'Coronation' class Pacifics were built, the first five Nos 6225-9 were streamlined as the first engines but were painted in a crimson lake and gilt livery. Here crimson No 6227 *Duchess of Devonshire* and blue No 6223 *Princess Alice* prepare to leave Polmadie shed before working southbound expresses on 29 August 1938. *T. G. Hepburn/Rail Archive Stephenson*

LOWER LEFT: No 6227 *Duchess of Devonshire* is seen again as it heads away from Northchurch Tunnel with the down 'Midday Scot' from Euston to Glasgow on 23 August 1938.
E. R. Wethersett/Real Photographs Co

TOP: The other five 'Coronation' class Pacifics built in 1938 Nos 6230-4 were not streamlined and are considered by many people to be the best looking engines ever built by the LMS. No 6231 *Duchess of Atholl* passes Willesden Junction with the down 'Midday Scot' on foggy 29 October 1938.
E. R. Wethersett/Real Photographs Co

ABOVE: No 6233 *Duchess of Sutherland* climbs away from Carlisle near Calthwaite with the up 'Midday Scot' in 1939. *E. E. Smith*

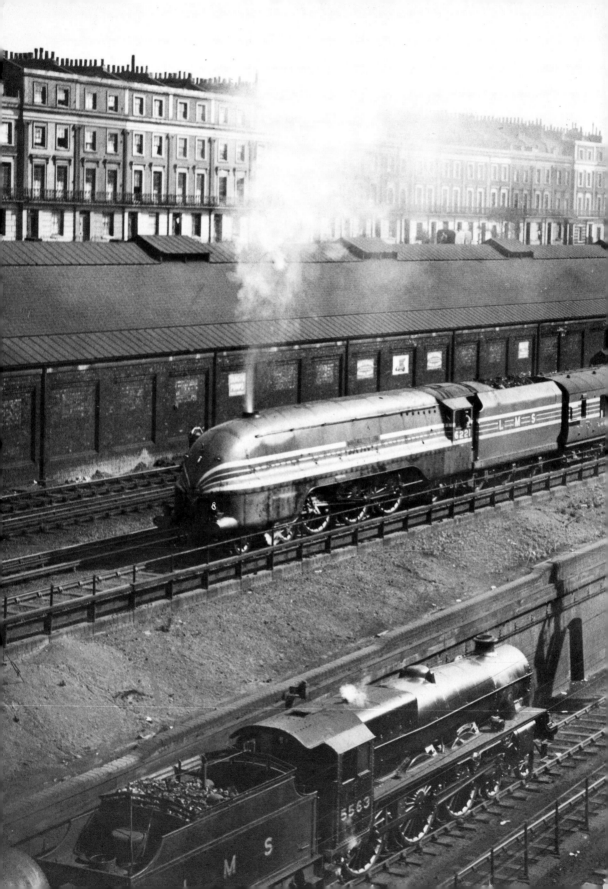

BELOW: The 'Coronation Scot' climbs Camden bank out of Euston behind
No 6221 *Queen Elizabeth* on 23 September 1938. In the foreground 'Jubilee' 4-6-0
No 5563 *Australia* backs up the hill to Camden shed.
E. R. Wethersett/Real Photographs Co

TOP: The last Pacific to be built to pure Stanier design was No 6255 *City of Hereford* seen climbing Camden bank with the Stranraer boat express from Euston in 1947. Two further engines of the class were built to a modified design by H. G. Ivatt. *F. R. Hebron/Rail Archive Stephenson*

ABOVE: In the period 1946-49 the streamlined casing was removed from those engines so fitted. Newly de-streamlined No 6222 *Queen Mary* is seen in the 1946 livery of black edged with maroon and straw. *W. H. Whitworth/Rail Archive Stephenson*

RIGHT: No 6254 *City of Stoke-on-Trent* departs from Carlisle with the 1.45pm Glasgow-Euston express on 20 April 1949 as the crew of 'Black Five' No 5450 look on. After experiments with a double chimney on No 6234 all engines from No 6235 were built with double chimneys and the earlier engines altered to conform. *Gavin L. Wilson*

ABOVE: 'Converted Royal Scot' Class 6P 4-6-0 No 6146 *The Rifle Brigade* passes Tring with a Liverpool-Euston express in 1947. The rebuilding of the 'Royal Scots' stemmed from the taper boiler rebuild of Fowler's high pressure 4-6-0 No 6399 *Fury* in 1935. *F. R. Hebron/Rail Archive Stephenson*

BELOW: 'Converted Royal Scot' 4-6-0 No 6122 *Royal Ulster Rifleman* climbs Camden bank with a Euston-Liverpool and Manchester express in 1947. It took from 1943 to 1955 to rebuild all the 'Royal Scots', 18 'Patriot' and two 'Jubilee' 4-6-0s were similarly rebuilt. *F. R. Hebron/Rail Archive Stephenson*

LEFT: In 1944 Charles Fairburn officially took over from Stanier as CME of the LMS though he had been acting in that capacity since 1942 when Stanier had been appointed to a government post to help the in the war effort. In 1945 Fairburn brought out his version of Class 4P 2-6-4T and a total of 277 were built. No. 2239 waits to leave Glasgow Central with a Burnside train in 1947. The final 41 engines of this class were built at Brighton by BR in 1950-51 for use on the Southern Region.
Gavin L. Wilson

BELOW: H. G. Ivatt took over as CME in 1945 for the final three years of the LMS. In that time he produced three new steam designs all of which were to continue under construction by BR. The final design to appear was his Class 4F 2-6-0 of which only three appeared in 1947 before the LMS was nationalised. No 3001 stands at Bletchley after arrival from Cambridge in April 1948.
P. Ransome-Wells

RIGHT: Introduced in 1946, H. G. Ivatt Class 2P 2-6-2T No 1205 leaves Idridgehay with an evening train for Wirksworth on 12 May 1947. A total of 130 of these snappy little engines were built, the last appearing in 1952. In BR days they were known as Class 2MT as was the tender engine version.
J. C. Flemons

BELOW: The tender engine version of H. G. Ivatt's 2-6-2T was the Class 2F 2-6-0 which first appeared in December 1946 and was built up to 1953 when 128 examples had been constructed. No 6402 is seen in Nottingham Midland station on 15 May 1948. *T. G. Hepburn/Rail Archive Stephenson*

ABOVE: On 12 December 1947 Britain's first main line diesel-electric locomotive was unveiled at Euston station. This was LMS No 10000, designed by H. G. Ivatt in collaboration with English Electric and was built at Derby. The 1,600bhp Co-Co passes Elstree with the 2.15pm St Pancras-Manchester express on 25 February 1948. It was joined by a sister No 10001 in 1948.
E. R. Wethersett/Rail Archive Stephenson